50 Simple Ways to Pamper Your Dog

Arden Moore

BARNES
&NOBLE
BOOKS
NEW YORK

2003 Barnes & Noble Books

ISBN 0-7607-3635-9

Printed and bound in the United States of America

03 04 05 06 07 08 MC 9 8 7 6 5 4 3 2 1

FG

Contents

 # Dedication

To all the wonderful and whimsical dogs
who have enriched my life
and taught me how to laugh.
Special mention goes to Crackers,
my childhood family dog,
and Mollie, my current four-legged pal.

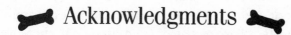 # Acknowledgments

I wish to thank all the veterinarians, animal behaviorists, dog trainers, animal shelter directors, and dog owners who generously shared their ideas in this book to make the world a much better place for our canine chums. Special thanks to my editor, Deborah Balmuth, for giving me this delightful opportunity to offer pampering tips to dog lovers everywhere.

Become Dog's Best Friend

Centuries ago, long before the invention of the leash, dogs agreed to become domesticated and serve the needs of our ancestors. They didn't balk, resist, or throw a tantrum. The dogs said, "Sure." They helped cavemen hunt for food, scooted rats out of 18th-century barns, and pulled cargo-laden sleds across frozen tundras. And what did they want in return? A big paycheck? Their names in lights? Naw, just a friendly pat on the head, a good meal, and a warm, dry place to sleep.

We've been on the receiving end of dog kindness for so, so long that we've come to expect canine catering. Well, I say enough! It's time we pamper our pooches the way they deserve.

I know. We all lead busy lives. The 40-hour work week went out with eight-track tapes. Family demands have escalated. With no time to shop, we order gifts over the Internet.

In the midst of this whirlwind patiently sit our love-you-forever dogs. Their tails are tapping. Their eyes are winking hellos. Their bodies are wiggling with delight.

This book will show you how to pamper your dog without booking an appointment. It's filled with simple, easy tips that you can seamlessly incorporate into your daily routine. Here's a way you can truly make it a dog's life.

Paws up!

Arden Moore

Think Like a Dog

When people meet, they exchange hand-shakes. When two dogs meet, they sniff each other. Same idea — totally different approach.

Person-to-person or dog-to-dog, different communication styles are used. We rely on the spoken word; dogs depend on scents and body posture cues. To bridge this communication gap and truly talk to dogs, you need to learn Dogspeak. That means you need to start thinking — even five minutes a day — like a dog. Put yourself in their paws for a moment. This is one of the best ways to pamper your dog.

Learning Dogspeak

Use these translation tips to keep yourself from committing a canine faux pas.

Dogs need to know where they rank in the family. They can be content to rank dead last as long as you consistently act like the leader of the pack. Few want to be pack leaders. Most want to feel safe.

Dogs "speak" in a rich vocabulary that consists of body language, vocal sounds, eye contact, and behavior. So, don't just listen to your dog's bark. You'll get his true message when you factor in body cues.

Pay attention to your tone more than your words. Dogs respond to intonations and body language. "Good boy" spoken in a harsh, low tone will be mistaken as a scolding by your dog.

Become a better "listener" by recognizing your dog's usual habits and expressions. Circular tail wagging is a friendly, let's-play signal among most dogs, while side-to-side wagging could be a welcome sign or a warning to back away.

Accept true dog affection. A dog who licks your face is conveying respect and "I love you" in Dogspeak.

Avoid direct eye contact when first meeting a dog, especially one that seems worried, high-strung, or aggressive. Staring can be misinterpreted as a threat or challenge. Instead, turn slightly away to expose your side or back to the dog until he feels more comfortable with your company.

THINGS WE CAN LEARN FROM OUR DOGS

We fill our days meeting work deadlines, maneuvering in traffic, and grocery shopping. What are priorities among canines? Let me illustrate with this anonymous gem found floating on the Internet:

- Run, romp, and play daily.
- If you want what lies buried, dig until you find it.
- When you're happy, dance around and wag your entire body.
- When it's in your best interest, practice obedience.
- Never pass up the opportunity to go for a joyride.
- Take naps and stretch before rising.

2

Bone Up on Your Bonding

Survey says . . . 90 percent of people consider their dogs to be full-fledged members of their families. Seventy-six percent feel guilty about leaving their dogs at home while they go to work, and 64 percent mention news about their dogs in their holiday cards. These statistics are encouraging, but we can improve the percentages by tightening the bonds we have with our dogs.

Bonding Like a Pro

Dogs are attracted to people who act in charge. Display an air of confidence. They look to you for clear direction and guidance. Don't be wishy-washy or deliver conflicting commands.

Practice unconditional love for your dog. Pamper her with lots of cuddling, friendly chatting, and playing. Give your dog your undivided attention in 5-minute spurts throughout the day.

Create a dog scrapbook starting with the first day your dog arrived at your home. Include photos, paw prints (my, how big you've grown!), and fun memories of adventures and events you shared. Sit down with your dog and paw through the pages together. He may not understand your words, but he will certainly know you're praising him.

Deliver plenty of verbal praise in an upbeat voice: "You're a great dog, a truly great dog." And don't forget to grin.

Stick to a routine as much as possible. Dogs are creatures of habit. Feed your dog at the same time each day. Try to take her on walks at scheduled times. A household routine helps make dogs feel more secure.

Did your dog win best of show for her looks or abilities? Why not spend that prize money by showering your winner with treats or toys? Or donate the prize money to your local animal shelter or favorite nonprofit animal organization.

Stage an event in your community that spotlights dogs. Arrange an annual Bark in the Park day in which dogs can be treated to pet massages, dog portraits, and fun games, such as musical chairs. Solicit participation from area animal shelters and pet product vendors.

For the TV-viewing dog, rent tail-wagging favorites from your video store. Not sure? Try these canine classics: *101 Dalmatians, The Adventures of Milo and Otis, Beethoven, Benji, Homeward Bound: The Incredible Journey,* and *My Dog Skip.* Also record pet shows on television. *Animal Planet* is my pal Mollie's favorite show — paws down!

Wear a lot of bright green or red clothes. These Christmas colors are the most visible hues to dogs.

Give your dog a pet name or two, or three. A friend of mine calls her Beagle (formally known as Daisy) "Boo Boo Bear," "Daisy Mae," and "Sweetie Pie." Daisy answers to all these affectionate terms.

A Home Fit for a Dog

Your home can also be your dog's castle — without a lot of renovation or expense. When you think about it, most dogs spend more time inside the house than you do, so they deserve some pleasing decor perks.

Play Decorator

Strategically place some comfy rugs on hardwood or tile floors to cushion the pressure points of napping dogs.

Open the blinds to allow warm sunshine to pour in and to give your dogs a good lookout spot for watching what's going on outside.

Why should cats get indoor bathroom facilities and not dogs? Some dog-conscious folks have created clever options for doggie bathrooms. There are doggie litter boxes available that are ideal for house training a puppy or providing relief for a senior dog with a weak bladder. One of my favorite inventions is a nifty portable toilet for the balcony — or anywhere inside the house — called the Patio Park. It features a 2- by 4-foot base, two strips of real grass sod, and a 22-inch-high splash guard that is easy to clean. Best of all, it takes only a few minutes to assemble, and the sod for this self-irrigating device can be replaced monthly. Inventor Joni MacLaine created this portable potty for her aging dog Sugar, who has bladder problems. For more information, contact the Patio Park company toll free at (877) 600-7429 or tap into its Web site: www.patiopark.com.

Drape throw blankets or cotton sheets over sofas and recliners so that your dog can snooze without depositing a mountain of hair on your upholstery.

Take away temptation by stashing kitchen garbage in heavy-lidded containers or inside a latched cabinet.

Keep a toy chest for all your dog's playthings. Bring out a few at a time to keep your dog occupied but not overwhelmed by the selection.

Place a dog bed in a busy area of the home, such as a corner of the kitchen or living room. The bed is your dog's refuge, but it also keeps her within sight of family activities inside the home. Dogs are social animals and don't like isolation.

Invest in a vacuum cleaner that has beater bars. This feature effectively sucks up fleas and fur. If you suspect you have a flea problem, always take the vacuum cleaner outside and discard the bag in an outdoor container (with a lid) after each sweep through the house.

Keep loose change in narrow-necked bottles to prevent accidental swallowing and choking episodes. Stash earrings, rings, cuff links, and necklaces in fastened jewelry boxes out of paw's reach.

Did you inherit Aunt Sally's antique vase? Put it in a safe place out of the path of a dodging, darting dog.

Place window stickers indicating the number of dogs you have to alert police or firefighters in case of an emergency, such as a house fire.

4

Bone-a-fide Healthy Herbs

Your garden may aptly serve as a backyard pharmacy for what ails and worries your dog. Herbs harbor the healing power of nature's oldest medicines, and their use dates back centuries. Active constituents inside a plant's flowers, petals, stems, and roots can be used to prevent or treat a variety of physical and emotional woes. Beyond the garden, supermarkets, drug stores, and health food stores stock medicinal herbs in tea, tincture, and capsule forms.

Natural Healing

Ever watch your dog chew grass? Does he like the taste? Maybe. Maybe not. Dogs most likely ingest grass because they instinctively know it will help them overcome a bout of indigestion.

Like the other members of our families, dogs deserve natural, safe treatments free of side effects whenever possible. But before giving your dog herbal medicine, always check with a holistic veterinarian or a member of the American Herbalists Guild at (435) 722-8434 or on the Web at www.healthy.net/herbalists.

Itchy-Skin Remedy

If your dog is suffering from itchy skin not caused by fleas, try this easy-to-make herbal concoction. Flower essences, which are available in most health food stores, are gentle healing remedies made from plants.

- 3 drops agrimony flower essence
- 3 drops beech flower essence
- 3 drops cherry plum flower essence
- 3 drops crab apple flower essence
- 3 drops walnut flower essence

Pour all of the flower essences into a small (4-ounce) plastic spray bottle. Fill it with spring water. Seal the top and shake vigorously. Spritz the itchy spots twice a day.

Using Herbs for Health

Here is a sampling of herbs for some common doggie conditions:

Allergies — chamomile, nettles, ox-eye daisy

Anxiety — passionflower, Rescue Remedy (a brand-name specialty flower essence mixture)

Arthritis — alfalfa, dandelion, devil's claw, parsley, yucca

Bleeding — cayenne, shepherd's purse

Burns and cuts, minor — aloe, calendula, St.-John's-wort

Constipation — plantain, senna, turmeric

Diarrhea — marsh mallow, slippery elm

Fleas — chaparral, sage, wormwood

Gas — chamomile, dill, fennel, peppermint

Hyperactivity — skullcap with chamomile or valerian

Indigestion — dill, hawthorn, marsh mallow, plantain, slippery elm

Infections (bacterial or viral) — cat's claw, echinacea, garlic

Motion sickness — ginger

Nervousness — hops, valerian

Skin problems — burdock, ginger, sage

Urinary infections — echinacea, marsh mallow, yarrow

chow Time

Chow time ranks as the number-one favorite activity of canines. For proof, just take a look at your dog when you pick up the empty food bowl. In anticipation, your dog will exhibit the telltale signs of "feed me": smacking lips, drooling mouth, begging paws, and full-body wiggling.

Cultivate Healthy Habits

Sure, you want to feed to please, but don't go overboard. If you truly want to pamper your dog at chow time, feed him the right amount of the right food. That's easier said than done. When two brown, soulful eyes are aimed your way, it's human nature to heap on the helpings. But resist and your dog will live a longer, healthier, and happier life. Here are some helpful hints for making mealtime a happy time for both of you.

Make your dog *think* she's getting more food. Instead of feeding her one big bowl once a day, divide the same amount of chow into three or four minimeals. Smaller, frequent meals are easier to digest and help your dog's metabolism work more efficiently.

Feed your dog in a room away from the dining room while you're enjoying your dinner. This prevents begging and allows you both to dine without interruption.

Make a drink on the rocks. Help your dog keep cool and occupied during warm days by giving him a few ice cubes to chew on. The crunchy cubes are fun to eat and provide essential fluids your dog needs to keep from overheating.

Switch to healthy treats, such as carrot sticks, instead of high-calorie, store-bought doggie jerky or sausage treats.

On special occasions, dole out these tasty treats: one meatball (minus the sauce), a small piece of cooked hamburger, 1 ounce (28 g) of boneless broiled chicken, or a dice-sized cube of hard cheese.

For dogs with sensitive stomachs, do what Leslie Sinclair, DVM, of Montgomery Village, Maryland, does for her greyhound, Moses: She warms up a veggie burger as a treat. She also occasionally gives Moses the crusts off her son's peanut-butter-and-whole-wheat sandwiches.

Mealtime can offer an assist with some minor medical conditions. Give doggie dandruff the brush-off by adding a teaspoon of corn, safflower, peanut, or sunflower oil to your dog's main meal of the day. These oils help replenish the body's natural oils and reduce dry, itchy skin.

Never buy low-fat dog food. Fat helps keep your dog's coat and skin looking healthy and provides energy. Just be sure not to give too much fat (ask your veterinarian for guidelines).

Check the expiration date on food labels and never serve your dog food that is past its prime.

Go easy on the cheese treats. Cheese is a great calcium source but too much can cause diarrhea.

Get rid of any food your dog leaves in the bowl after mealtime. Clean the bowl to prevent the growth of bacteria, such as *E. coli* or salmonella. Once a week, put your dog's food and water bowls into the dishwasher for a thorough cleaning.

Respond to begging by taking your dog for a walk, playing a game of fetch, or grooming instead of handing out food. Feed your dog at the same time you eat or usher him to another part of the house while you are eating.

WHAT TO LOOK FOR IN A DOG FOOD

Reading the dog food label will help you determine the percentage of protein, fat, and fiber. The guaranteed analysis on the label provides only the minimum percentage of crude protein and fat and the maximum amount of fiber and moisture. For peace of mind, choose food sanctioned by the Association of American Feed Control Officers (AAFC). The AAFC seal indicates the product has passed its rigorous feeding trials for balanced nutrition.

Be a discriminating dog food purchaser. Your dog will benefit from food containing these ingredients: vitamin E, beta-carotene, gamma linolenic acid, omega-3 fatty acids, proteins, fiber, glucosamines, L-carnitines, and chondroitin sulfates.

These substances help repair cartilage, rejuvenate dry skin, build muscle tissue, boost the immune system, and aid digestion.

Did you know that small dogs burn more calories than do large dogs, ounce for ounce? Were you aware that older, less active dogs need fewer calories and that working dogs burn more calories than their couch-lounging counterparts? Factor in your dog's age, weight, activity level, flavor preferences, and health when selecting commercial dog food.

Sprinkle in some treats with the dry food in self-feeders so when your dog munches she occasionally gets a tasty tidbit.

Serve food and water at your dog's eye level. Put chow in elevated bowls or on top of low tables or crates so that your dog won't strain his neck and back muscles. Elevated chow counters also help your dog digest better.

For dogs that like to nibble all day, consider automatic feeders that dispense the amount of dry food and water you specify.

Don't serve food or water in plastic bowls. Chew-prone dogs can perforate edges, inviting bacteria to thrive.

6

Be Down in the Mouth

Don't dismiss doggie breath. That odious odor could be an early warning sign of gingivitis or other dental problems. In fact, 80 percent of dogs lacking dental care develop gum and teeth problems by age three, according to the American Veterinary Dental Society.

Care for Those Pearly Whites

Look inside your dog's mouth at least twice a week and check for signs of deterioration, especially bleeding gums, pale gums, persistent foul breath, tartar buildup, decay, sores, or broken or missing teeth.

Provide fresh water daily. Bacteria can build up inside bowls containing water that is more than two days old.

Feed your dog a raw carrot to help scrub away plaque. It's also a good source of vitamins A and C and fiber.

Avoid giving your dog real bones. You'll run the risk of splinters with sharp edges that can cut a dog's mouth and intestinal lining.

To get your dog used to the brushing routine, break it down into a few steps done over a series of brushing sessions. Dip your finger into beef bouillon and then rub the finger gently over her mouth and teeth. Gradually add gauze over your finger and gently scrub the teeth in a circular motion. Finally, introduce a soft toothbrush designed for dogs and use meat-flavored toothpaste.

Schedule a yearly professional dental cleaning to get rid of stubborn tartar. The vet can also look for any tooth damage and make necessary repairs.

7

Scent-sational Vacations

Traveling with your dog is one time when you need to map out a detailed itinerary in advance — for your dog's sake. As cute and sweet as your dog may be to you, not everyone welcomes dogs with open arms. Plan to visit places that are dog friendly and interesting to both you and your canine.

Where to Go?

Before you two hop in the car for that long road trip, contact the State Department of Tourism for each state you plan to visit. The phone numbers are available from directory assistance for each capital city. They can help you find vacation spots and hotels that put out the welcome mat for dogs.

Solicit the help of a travel agent in booking your vacation with your dog. If you're a member of the American Automobile Association, your local chapter can assist.

Hmmm . . . where would your dog like to visit? Why not state parks? These natural wonderlands provide plenty of spots for walking and hiking. Or head for national parks. Many of them, including Yellowstone and the Mall in Washington, D.C., permit leashed dog visitors. The list of dog-welcoming places can be found by searching the National Park Service at www.nps.gov.

BACK TO BASICS

Camping with dogs is pleasurable whether it's an overnight stay or a two-week outing. This activity traces its roots back centuries, when humans and dogs hunted for food together and shared campfires. Fresh air and new sights, sounds, and smells await your pooch, not to mention paddling in lakes and rivers. Consider your dog's size, age, health, and attitude when deciding on a camping adventure so that it is fun for both of you.

8

Crate Mates

Choosing the perfect crate for your canine can be as challenging as selecting a cup of coffee these days. There are oodles of styles in varying price ranges. What's a dog owner to do? Before you whip out the credit card at your local pet store, take the following factors into consideration.

Crate Savvy

Choose a crate that is just big enough to allow your dog to stand up straight, turn around, and lie down. Bigger is not better. The general rule is that the crate should not exceed one and a half times the size of your dog.

Invest in a good, sturdy crate; it will reap dividends in the long run. Don't go for a bargain buy.

Always regard the crate as a haven for comfort or privacy. Never use it as a "temporary prison" for misbehavior. Your dog should view the crate as a safe, friendly place in which to sleep and spend time when you can't supervise closely.

Personalize your dog's crate with a couple of favorite toys. Leave the crate door open during the day so your dog can come and go at will.

Line the bottom of the crate with layers of newspapers and replace soiled papers often for toilet-training puppies.

Put the crate in an area with good air circulation.

Insert a soft pet bed or thick cushion on the bottom of the crate. Older dogs with joint problems or dogs that spend a lot of time in crates can benefit from the added support and comfort of 3-inch-thick orthopedic foam cushions.

Buy some soft fleece material from a sewing supply store. Cut it to fit the size of the crate floor.

The Ins and Outs of Doggie Doors

Free yourself from doorman duty! Give your well-behaved dog some freedom of movement by installing a doggie door. Your dog will be free to come and go inside the home and out into an enclosed backyard.

Coming and Going

There are many door designs suited to all types of home construction. They can be installed in existing doors or walls or set up as separate panels that act as extensions to sliding glass doors.

The doggie door of choice should be taller and wider than your dog. A plastic flap door works well in mild climates but won't barricade against very cold or warm weather. If you use the plastic-flap style, make sure it is flexible, safe, and nontoxic.

Determine which locking system works best for you and your dog. There are magnetic locks, latching locks, and electronic locks. Your dog can be fitted with an electronic device in the collar that permits only her to enter or leave the house; this prevents the occasional neighborhood dog from casually stopping over for an unannounced visit.

Build up your dog's confidence by leaving the flap or door off at first. Have someone stay inside with your dog while you go outside. Call your dog to come through the hole and praise him lavishly and give him a food treat. Once he has the hang of it, add the door and follow the same steps.

THE BENEFITS OF DOGGIE DOORS

Doggie doors help in the behavior department, too. If your dog learns to use a pet door, he will be less apt to destructively chew or dig to release stress. Same goes for excessive barking, door scratching, or accidental puddles inside the house.

Pet-i-cure, Please

Long nails are definitely not in fashion in the dog world. Clipping your dog's nails can be easy and quick with the right approach and tools. Treat your dog to regular pedicures to avoid snags in the carpet, infections, or injuries.

Painless Clipping Routines

Touch, tickle, and massage your dog's feet daily. This gets her used to having her paws handled and reduces her anxiety the first time you clip her nails.

Make nail clipping a happy event by beginning these stress-free manicures when your dog is a puppy. Do it in a quiet, confined place to eliminate any distractions — or escape routes.

Speak in a calm, reassuring tone during the clipping. Cut one nail the first time, and gradually, as your dog learns to accept the clipping without fussing, work your way to all four feet. Always finish trimming tasks with praise and a treat.

Use clippers that are specifically designed for dogs. These clippers do the job better and safer than the clippers you use on your own nails.

Clip your dog's nails after a bath or a swim, when the nails are soft.

If your dog has clear nails, trim just above the "quick" area. That's the pinkish part of the nail, and it contains blood vessels. If your dog has dark nails, just nip off the end every two weeks.

Keep a styptic pencil or styptic powder within reach in case you accidentally cut too deeply and cause bleeding. If you're temporarily out of a styptic product, sprinkle some cornstarch on the injured toe to stop the bleeding.

Brush Up Your Grooming Skills

With the exception of a few breeds, dogs shed a lot. It's one of life's certainties. That means you should expect to find dog hair on your furniture, along the baseboards, and in the rugs.

Brushing your dog's coat promotes a healthy shedding process, because it not only removes loose hair but also stimulates the skin. And regular brushing will leave your dog's coat shining.

Grooming to the Rescue!

Short of shaving your dog, here are some strategies to pamper your pet and prevent your home from turning into one giant ball of fur.

For the first brushing session, use a soft-bristled brush. Call your dog in a cheery tone and reward him with a small treat. Swab some peanut butter or soft cheese on the facing wall at his eye level. While he stands and licks, brush gently and provide plenty of praise.

Start on the surface of your dog's coat and gently work deeper to prevent the brush from getting trapped in tangles or clumps.

Practice Brush Hygiene

Treat your dog's brush with the same respect you lavish on yours. Remove excess hair from the brush with an old comb. Once a week, soak the brush in a sink filled with warm water and 2 tablespoons of shampoo. Rub the soapy mixture into the bristles and let the brush soak for 5 minutes. Rinse thoroughly with warm water and add a little white vinegar to get rid of any soap residue.

Always brush in the direction of fur growth. Going against the grain can irritate the skin and make your dog want to flee the scene when you pull out the grooming supplies. Use straight strokes for longhaired breeds; circular motions can break hair.

Loosen a shedding coat with a blow dryer. Turn it to a low, cool setting to avoid burning the skin, and brush gently to remove loose fur.

If your dog will tolerate it, adjust a vacuum cleaner to reduce the suction. Run the upholstery brush over your dog's coat to catch all the loose hair. Slip a piece of old pantyhose over the head of the brush with the bristles poking through. Simply pull off the pantyhose when you're finished brushing for easy cleanup.

Select grooming tools best suited to your dog's coat. Longhaired dogs prefer a shedding tool with serrated edges. This tool helps catch excess fur on the surface of the coat. Shorthaired dogs prefer a rubber currycomb. Its rounded nubs remove loose hair while massaging the skin.

After a thorough brushing, treat your dog's skin and coat to a dab of aloe to restore moisture.

12

Making the Skies Friendlier

You can make the skies friendly for your four-legged friend. Here are some ways to pilot a happy takeoff and smooth landing.

Take Off!

Schedule an appointment with your veterinarian within 10 days of the scheduled flight. Most airlines require up-to-date medical certificates verifying that your dog is healthy enough to make the trip and is current on all necessary inoculations.

Attach your address and phone number and ID tags to your dog's collar. Paste your name, dog's name, address, and phone number on the outside of the crate and carry the dog's ID info in your carry-on luggage. You can never have too much identification when it comes to your airborne dog!

Bring a current photograph of your dog with you. If he gets lost in the airport or at the destination, the photograph can make the search go much more smoothly.

Book early. A dog under 15 pounds may be able to ride with you in the passenger section on some airlines. Check before finalizing a reservation. Some airlines limit the number of pets per flight to two or three. Most make pet reservations on a first come, first serve basis. The crate must be able to slide easily under the seat in front of you. Acceptable airline carriers are 23 inches long by 13 inches wide by 9 inches high.

Walk your dog just before going to the check-in gate and immediately after you land.

For medium- to large-sized dogs who must travel in the baggage compartments, invest in a heavy-duty, secure crate. The best and safest choice is a noncollapsible crate (some are made of aluminum and others of a plastic-aluminum combination).

Size up your dog. The crate should be just big enough for your dog to lie down, stand up, and turn around easily. Don't think bigger is better. Too much wiggle room and the dog can be bounced against the crate wall or become chilled.

Store the leash inside your carry-on luggage, not inside the crate. This eliminates the possibility that your dog will get caught or choked or that the leash will spill out of the crate.

Avoid putting food in the crate. The ride can be upsetting for some dogs, which can lead to digestive problems.

Place ice cubes in the water tray of the crate.

Select the time of your flight on the basis of weather conditions. For example, avoid flying in the middle of the day during hot summers.

Pack some paper towels in your carry-on and also in the crate, if there is a slot available. The towels are helpful in case of a doggie accident.

Seek direct flights to avoid accidental transfers or delays. Always travel on the same flight as your dog.

Consult your veterinarian about tranquilizers or relaxing herbs for your dog. Some breeds with short noses, including pugs and boxers, are prone to breathing difficulties and may not be good candidates for tranquilizers, which can impair respiratory functions.

Be a scrutinizing airline shopper. Make sure that the airplane has ventilation in class D. This is the class that represents the compartment for transporting live animals and baggage. Airlines are not required to provide ventilation by law — yet.

Place a warm blanket inside the pet carrier or crate to keep your dog from suffering chills during winter flights. The cargo area is unheated and can get quite cold.

BE CIVIC MINDED

Lobby your legislator to make the skies even friendlier for your dog. Congress recently attached the "pets on planes" amendment to the Federal Administration reauthorization bill. This bill requires airlines to report all incidents of loss, injury, or death and to provide training for airline employees on how to handle traveling pets. It also requires retrofitting airplane cargo areas for adequate temperature and ventilation control.

Need an Acupuncture Needle?

The ancient Chinese practice of acupuncture dates back centuries. This painless treatment is based on the philosophy that disease is the consequence of the body's energy, or *qi,* being out of balance. Acupuncture restores energy balance by inserting special tiny needles strategically along meridians in the skin. These meridians correspond to different areas of the body, including the heart, the lungs, and the liver.

Know the Facts

Acupuncture activates various sensory receptors in the body. These receptors control temperature, pain, and pressure. Some receptors also stimulate nerves that send impulses to the brain to release endorphins, the body's natural painkilling hormones. Acupuncture leads to improved circulation, better muscle tone and tension, and a stronger immune system.

Acupuncture can complement — but not replace — traditional veterinary care. It is important to seek out qualified professionals. Fortunately, you have a terrific resource in the International Veterinary Acupuncture Society (IVAS), based in Longmont, Colorado. This professional organization represents more than 900 certified veterinarians. You can also check with the American Veterinary Medication Association (AVMA) at (847) 925-8070 or on the Web at www.avma.org.

Cost-wise, the national average ranges from $65 to $100 for an initial acupuncture visit and from $35 to $65 for subsequent sessions averaging 30 minutes.

Acupuncture is not a cure-all. It works best for chronic conditions, such as back pain, asthma, and allergies, but it's not recommended for pregnant dogs because it can induce labor. Also, acupuncture is not a good choice for dogs with high fevers. They usually need antibiotics to tackle bacterial infections.

A close cousin to acupuncture is acupressure, which relies on strategic placement of the fingertips along key meridians in the dog's body. No needles are used. For instance, the pressure point BL60 is located on the outside of the rear ankle. Press this spot between your thumb and index finger for 60 seconds once or twice a day to help improve blood flow in dogs, especially ones with arthritis.

Lord, let me be the person that my dog thinks I am.

— Unknown

14

Make Fleas Flee

One pair of mating fleas can produce 20,000 offspring in just three months! Fleas can also last several months without a blood meal. Combine these two factors and you'll understand why your dog can become a four-legged smorgasbord for these pervasive pests.

Prevention Is the Cure

One of the best ways to pamper your dog is to make him flea free. You may not always be able to prevent fleas from entering your home, but you can take aggressive steps to avoid infestation.

Groom your dog two or three times a week with a tiny-tined flea comb. Dip the comb in hot, soapy water or a dish of rubbing alcohol diluted in water. Either method will drown fleas.

Wash your dog's bedding and throw rugs from high pet traffic areas once a week, in hot water, to rid them of any fleas.

Suck up fleas with a vacuum cleaner that features a beater bar. This model can bag adult fleas, larvae, and eggs. Once you're done, seal the bag and throw it in an outside garbage can with a lid.

When you bathe your dog, leave the sudsy flea shampoo on her for 10 minutes for the best effect. Distract her by singing songs or playing music in the bathroom. Or put a tablespoon of peanut butter on the wall facing your dog so she can lick it off while she's waiting.

Don't forget to wash your dog's favorite chew toys, her collar, and her leash in hot, soapy water once a week to get rid of any flea eggs.

Crush a fresh clove of garlic into your dog's food at each meal. This aromatic herb won't kill fleas, but it effectively acts as nature's flea repellent.

Fight back with pyrethrin. This safe, natural insecticide is derived from the chrysanthemum plant and kills adult fleas. Look for this ingredient in flea shampoos, dips, sprays, and powders. Or use its synthetic version, known as pyrethroid.

Bomb fleas with borate. This powder kills flea larvae that nest in your carpets and upholstery. Apply the powder once a year or every time you have your carpets professionally cleaned.

Stash some cedar shavings inside the washable cover of your dog's bedding. Fleas detest the smell.

Roust them with rotenone. This natural insecticide kills adult fleas. It is derived from the root of the plant *Derris ellipta.* Look for rotenone in shampoos, sprays, and rinses. *Note:* Do not use this substance on puppies or old dogs.

Provide a high-quality diet. My holistic veterinarian agrees that fleas prefer sickly dogs to dogs that get healthy chow and plenty of exercise.

15

There's the Rub!

Dogs know instinctively how to stretch properly. Notice that they stretch when they first awaken and that they do tail-to-nose stretches several times during the day. Stretching reduces muscle tension and stiffness, and it improves circulation of blood and lymph. It enhances flexibility and range of motion. Stretching also makes dogs less prone to injury.

Simple Stretching Techniques

My friend C. Sue Furman, Ph.D., a canine massage instructor as well as a professor of anatomy and neurobiology at Colorado State University in Fort Collins, Colorado, highly recommends that dog owners learn how to treat their pets to regular sessions of passive stretching to promote range of motion.

To begin, place your dog on his side on a carpet or padding in a quiet place without distractions. Then follow this sequence:

Step 1. Hold the front leg above and below the elbow for optimal support.

Step 2. Raise the front leg toward the head slowly. Hold the position for 5 seconds.

Step 3. Stretch the front leg toward the tail. Stop at the point of resistance and hold for 5 seconds.

Step 4. Repeat steps 1 through 3 on the other front leg, and then with each of the back legs.

Step 5. Gradually increase the holding time to 10 to 15 seconds.

Massage Dos and Don'ts

Once you have spoiled your dog with stretching, you're ready to become his personal masseuse. Massage is a hot trend among dog-loving folks who realize the medical, bonding, and behavioral benefits of providing just the right therapeutic touch for their canines.

Here are some dos and don'ts:

- 🐾 **Do** approach your dog slowly and speak in a soothing tone.
- 🐾 **Do** let your dog pick the time and place.
- 🐾 **Do** wash your hands and keep them free of oils, creams, or lotions.
- 🐾 **Do** massage only with your hands and never your feet — no matter how talented your toes are!
- 🐾 **Do** pay attention to your dog's feedback. If he hangs around, gives you a sleepy glance, or falls asleep, you've got the right touch. If he starts wiggling, resisting, and trying to escape, end the session.
- 🐾 **Do** look for lumps, swellings, cuts, fleas, or ticks. Alert your veterinarian should these conditions continue or worsen.
- 🐾 **Do** stroke the muscles toward the heart to enhance healthy blood flow.
- 🐾 **Do** enroll in a canine massage class. The best instructors are licensed massage therapists with certification in dog massage.
- 🐾 **Don't** press too deeply.
- 🐾 **Don't** give a massage when you're feeling stressed. Dogs read your body cues.
- 🐾 **Don't** pat your dog on the top of the head. Switch to smooth, soothing strokes.
- 🐾 **Don't** directly massage an open wound or the site of recent surgery. Gently massage above and below the area to stimulate blood flow, which will increase the supply of nutrients needed for repair and healing.

16

Let Sleeping Dogs Lie

How many of us have nudged, even shoved, a snoring spouse, but endured many a restless night rather than touch a single hair on our bed-hogging, snoring dog?

Dogs in dreamland capture our hearts. Never mind that they sleep nearly twice as many hours a day as we do. Here are some ways to pamper your snoozing dog.

Dreamy Delights

Place rectangular-shaped pillows on hard floors to make them cushy and comfy for afternoon siestas.

Cure your dog of blanket stealing by enticing him to sleep on a new foam doggie bed. First, remove the cover of the doggie bed and give it a thorough washing and drying. Then, tuck it between your bedspread and top sheet. Let it remain there a few days to collect your scent, then put the cover back on the doggie bed and lure your dog to it with a treat or favorite toy. In no time, he will love this snoozing spot because it reminds him of you.

Position your dog's bed in a warm, cozy spot away from drafts.

Toss a blanket in the dryer for 10 to 15 minutes and drape it over your dog during chilly nights. This will help her fall asleep, and the dry heat eases joint aches and increases flexibility.

Let sleeping dogs enter dream cycles undisturbed. Yes, dogs do dream. Scientific research has discovered that small dogs dream more frequently than large dogs, but large dogs enjoy longer dreams.

When you're ready to awaken your dog, whisper her name. This is an important stimulus detected by the dog's subconscious mind. Allow your dog's eyes to open before touching her body so you don't startle her. Let your dog stand up, stretch, and jump down from the bed or chair on her own.

17

Puppy Charm School

Yes, it's true: As cute as puppies are, they must be taught how to socialize. The prime learning time is between 4 and 14 weeks of age. This is your golden opportunity to instill good manners, self-confidence, and trust in the newest addition to your family.

During this period, your goal should be to expose your impressionable puppy to big dogs, little dogs, happy dogs, and playful dogs. He should meet tall people and short people. People who speak with accents and those who wear hats. Young people. Old people. Yes, even c-a-t-s!

Your puppy also needs to get used to his surroundings so that he doesn't develop unfounded fears. Let him get used to the sound of the vacuum cleaner, the dishwasher, the dryer, and the lawn mower. Introduce him to his reflection in mirrors. Under your careful supervision, place him on different surfaces and heights. Hoist him up on the slick dryer top (the surface simulates a veterinary clinic's exam table) and let him paw through a gravel driveway.

Fortunately, animal behaviorists and trainers recognize the value of socialization. All over the country, puppy charm schools are popping up. Check with your local humane society or pet store for a school in your area. The classes usually meet weekly. Your puppy must be current on all health shots before enrolling.

Raising Your "Little One" Right

In addition to these formal schools, you can do your part to ensure that your puppy grows up to be a happy, well-adjusted dog. Consider these good parenting tips.

Put mirrors in your dog's play area so he gets used to himself.

Knot a clean old dish towel, wet it, and let it chill in the freezer. Give it to your teething puppy to massage her tender gums. Don't worry: Make the knot big and your puppy can't swallow it.

Cradle your puppy instead of carrying him to prevent the squirming youngster from falling. Use both hands to pick up your puppy. Place one hand under his chest just behind his forelegs. Put the other hand under his belly. Lift and cradle his hind legs in one arm and let his forelegs rest on your other arm for comfort and support.

Make your hand a friend to your dog. Never hit your puppy or she will learn to mistrust hands and may become fear aggressive.

Distract your puppy when he's headed for mischief so that he learns success rather than failure. Always reward him for doing what you asked.

Avoid long, drawn-out goodbyes. About 5 minutes before leaving home, give your puppy something to gnaw on, like a hollow rubber toy with peanut butter stuffed into its opening. Walk out the door without saying a word. Don't make a big to-do when you return home or you can cause your dog to become hyperactive and destructive as a result of separation anxiety.

18

Respect Your Elder Dogs

Treat your aging dog like a VIP — a Very Important Pooch. The graying of his muzzle, the slowing of his step should be signals to increase your amount of pampering. Your dog has been loyal to you since puppyhood. Now it's time to show him some extra appreciation.

The Golden Years

Here are some ways you can help your dog age gracefully.

Place water bowls in different locations inside the house. Older dogs tend to drink less. With water readily available, your dog is less likely to become dehydrated. Measure all the water levels regularly to determine how much your dog is drinking.

For your arthritic dog, provide glucosamine capsules to improve mobility. This supplement stimulates production of synovial fluid, the body's natural joint lubricant. Ask your vet for more information.

Treat your dog to a chewable pet vitamin as a reward. These vitamins provide many important nutrients your aging dog needs.

On or around your dog's seventh birthday, give the best present that can't be wrapped in a gift box: a comprehensive vet checkup that includes blood and urine samples. The lab-analyzed results will provide a baseline of your dog's condition and help your veterinarian customize her care.

Continue daily exercise. Dogs that are regularly walked a minimum of 20 minutes a day since puppyhood are less likely to develop age-related disorders or digestive problems. Regular, moderate exercise such as swimming tones muscles without putting added stress on the arthritic joints.

Keep your older dog on a leash during walks, especially at night. As the years pass, your dog's hearing and vision may fade. You need to hone your senses to keep your dog out of harm's way.

Elevate food and water bowls so your dog doesn't have to lower his head to eat and drink.

Keep your dog's sleeping area warm and cozy. Apply a warm water bottle or towel over arthritic joints. Massage the area with gentle circular motions.

Install ramps to help your dog climb up stairs, into the car, or up on the bed. The best ramps are wide enough to meet the dog's needs and feature nonslip surfaces for greater traction. You can also make your own from a foam-core surfboard (it is light but sturdy). Cover it with rubber mesh — the type installed under rugs to keep them from slipping. The slight curve of the surfboard easily fits over the doorstep, and the rubber mesh provides a nonslip surface. Select one that is 19 inches wide and 42 inches long, a size that can accommodate most dogs.

19

Ain't Misbehavin'

No dog is perfect. For that matter, no person is either. Don't strive for perfection in your canine pal. Instead, practice what my animal behaviorist friends call "redirection." If your dog is up to mischief, call his name to get his attention. Then distract him from the misdeed by enticing him with a more appropriate — and dog-pleasing — action. You will both feel happier.

Distraction Tactics

Some dogs just gotta dig. It's in their genetic makeup. So, divert them from your prized petunias, herbal garden, or vegetable plot by dedicating a place in your backyard that welcomes the dig-minded dog. Build him his very own sandbox. Depending on the size of the dog and your backyard, a 3- or 4-foot square area may be just dandy. See the box on page 54 for more information.

What do you do with a yapping dog? Reward silence. Dogs are master manipulators. If you rush up to them and shout every time they go on a barking spree, they quickly realize this is a great ploy for attention. Instead, praise your dog warmly when he does his best mime impression. Give him a few scratches behind the ear or another favorite spot or hand-deliver a small treat. Also, exercise your pal often with brisk, long walks and intense play sessions to tucker him out and make him want to sleep, not bark.

Can't break your dog's habit of chewing your sunglasses? Buy him his own pair of designer shades. Some pet catalogs and stores carry doggie-chew sunglasses in wild colors. He can be a cool dude as he drools.

You can also stop a vocalizing dog in midbark with just a few "common cents." Put a handful of pennies into a rinsed soda can. Seal the opening with some duct tape. The next time your dog goes on a yapping spree, say "Hush" and give the can a few vigorous shakes. The noise should startle the dog enough to silence him.

MAKING A SANDBOX

To create a sandbox for your dog, choose a square area in your backyard. Remove the sod and dig down at least 18 inches. Remove the dirt, yank out the roots, and pluck out rocks and other debris. Then fill the hole with sand or soft dirt. Introduce your dog to his new digs by tossing a hard biscuit on top. Praise him when he scampers off to get it and eat it. Tuck a second biscuit 6 inches under the sand and encourage him to dig for this tasty buried treasure. You can also hide your dog's favorite toy 6 inches under and tell him to go find it. Before you know it, your dog will be enjoying this new game in his sandbox. If he happens to stray back to your gardens, tell him "No" and redirect him back to his sandbox with a toy or biscuit. He will soon learn that there are more perks and prizes in his sandbox than your garden plots.

Your new puppy makes your heart melt — and your table legs wobbly. His need to gnaw escalates during the teething phase of puppyhood. Save your furniture and promote good dental habits by smearing hollow rubber toys with peanut butter, soft cheese, or even chicken fat or bacon grease. Any of these flavors is a whole lot more appealing to your puppy's taste buds than bare wood. You can also use bitter-flavored chewing deterrents, which are sold in most pet stores.

Stop puppy chewing with chicken broth ice cubes. Roll a few cubes onto the kitchen floor so that your teething puppy can chew and soothe her sore gums.

Instead of constantly trying to shoo your dog off the furniture, try sealing off the room with a mesh-covered gate in the doorway. This way, your dog can still see and will not feel penned behind a closed door. Or protect your furniture with a washable throw blanket or cotton sheet that you can remove once you return home. This is a win-win situation for both of you.

20

Paws-itively Fun Indoor Games

free bones!

When it's raining cats and dogs outside or the snow is knee-high to a St. Bernard, be a good foul-weather friend to your dog by playing games indoors. Pick a room with enough space for tail-wagging romps and stash the breakables out of paw's reach.

Intermingle tricks and games with a few reinforcing obedience commands and you'll have a fun-loving dog with good manners. Let the games begin!

Quick Tricks

Teach your dog to behave like a Houdini hound. Hold a small treat or ball in one closed fist and keep the other fist empty. Extend both arms out and ask your dog, "Which hand?" Let him sniff both. When he noses the fist with the toy or food, open it, show him, and praise him. Repeat, randomly moving the toy or food into your left or right hand. Now you're both ready for an audience!

Play hide and seek. Have your dog heel by your side in a room. Throw a treat across the room. As your dog darts after it, slip around the corner out of sight and call your dog by name. When she races to you, reward her with a treat and plenty of praise. Repeat four or five times.

Have him "find the keys." Stash the keys on the couch, under a chair, or in your dog's bed. When he brings them to you, reward him with a treat. Then stash them in a new place and repeat the retrieve-and-get-a-treat steps.

Play "get the remote control." Dogs like jobs. While having your dog fetch the remote brings out the true couch potato in you, it gives your dog a mission. When she brings you the remote, reward her with a treat and plenty of praise. Then sit down and enjoy a good canine caper together — perhaps *Frasier* or *Lassie* reruns.

21

Support the Spay Way

The birth of a litter of puppies is certainly a miracle to behold. But it's time for a reality check: There are simply not enough homes for all. Show true compassion for the dogs of the world by having your dog spayed (for females) or neutered (for males) before 6 months of age.

Be a Pal

If you have your veterinarian spay your female dog before her first heat (estrus) cycle, you're doing her a terrific favor. Spaying dramatically reduces her risk of developing uterine infections, ovarian cancer, and breast cancer.

As for the boys, neutered males have far fewer prostate problems (including cysts, abscesses, and prostate cancer) than do unaltered males, and they can't develop testicular cancer. They are less likely to roam, fight, demonstrate aggressiveness, or display hyperactive behavior.

Schedule the surgical appointment early in the day so that you can pick your dog up in the early evening (unless your vet recommends an overnight stay). Also, select a time when you will be home for a couple of days after the surgery — weekends are good — so that you can provide comfort and reassurance to your healing friend.

The one absolutely unselfish friend that man can have in this selfish world, the one that never deserts him, the one that never proves ungrateful or treacherous, is his dog.

— George Graham Vest

TOP 10 REASONS TO SPAY OR NEUTER YOUR DOG

1. Altered dogs, on average, live longer, healthier lives.
2. Female dogs spayed before their first birthday are 99.9 percent less likely to develop reproductive cancer.
3. Altered dogs behave better and are more focused on training.
4. You'll stop overpopulation. One female dog and her offspring can produce 67,000 dogs in just six years.
5. You'll stop homelessness. Only one in four dogs finds a permanent, loving home.
6. You'll stop the killings. More than eight million surplus dogs and cats are destroyed each year because there are not enough homes for them. Taxpayers pick up the tab to the tune of $300 million.
7. Eighty percent of dogs struck by vehicles are unaltered males.
8. The majority of dog bites to postal carriers are from unaltered male dogs.
9. Pet licensing fees are lower in cost for altered dogs in many cities and counties.
10. Thanks to improved surgical and anesthesia equipment and techniques, you can spay a female or neuter a male as early as 8 weeks of age. Don't hesitate.

22

Is There a Vet in the House?

Y ou are the front line of defense for shielding your dog from many diseases and injuries. Even though your vet visits may be only once or twice a year, there are lots of steps you can take at home to prevent problems.

At-Home Doctoring

Weigh your dog weekly. Any substantial shifts — gains *or* losses — can be a clue to an underlying problem. Record the weights and report any major deviations to your vet. Train giant breeds to walk on a weight mat available at pet stores.

Give your dog a thorough head-to-tail checkup at least once a week. And don't forget to check her eyes, ears, and mouth. Your observations may help catch a disease during its early stages.

Dogs detest taking pills, but you can make the medicine go down easier. The quickest way is to insert the pill into a ball of moist dog food and give it to your dog as a treat. Follow with a doggie biscuit to make sure that the pill was swallowed.

If your dog keeps spitting out the pill, try plan B: Open his jaws wide and pop the pill on top of his tongue as far back as possible. Then hold his jaws closed and massage his throat. Try blowing a quick puff of air into his face. When he blinks, he automatically swallows.

If the first two pill-giving tricks don't work, try plan C: Insert the pill into the center of a grape and give it as a treat. Get the taste of the pill out of your dog's taste buds with several more grapes.

Hire a mobile groomer to come to your home for your car-terrified canine. Most feature stainless steel tubs with hot and cold water, hydraulic grooming tables, high-velocity dryers, and vacuum systems.

Check your dog's pulse. It's easy to do and strengthens your bond through touch. Recognize that the smaller the dog, the faster the pulse. A normal resting heart rate for a small dog ranges between 140 and 160 beats per minute; for a medium dog, between 120 and 140; and for a large dog, between 60 and 80.

Give your dog baby food during mild bouts of diarrhea. Dogs really go for poultry and lamb. Stick with meat flavors — vegetables can make the diarrhea worse. A small dog can eat one jar a day; a medium dog, two; and a large dog, three. If diarrhea persists for more than three days, check with your vet, as your dog is at risk for dehydration.

How to Take a Pulse

1. Position your dog on his side.
2. Slide your hand under the top back leg.
3. Feel for the crease where the body meets the leg.
4. Place your index and middle fingers along the groove where the artery is located.
5. Count the pulse for a minute. Or measure a 20-second pulse and multiply by 3.

23

Safety Rules

O ur dogs are viable members of the family. Just as we do our best to look out for our children, we need to practice safety precautions for our faithful, fun-loving dogs. Here are ways to reduce the risk of harm to your dog.

Learning to Be Careful

Treat your dog like a toddler. Both are naturally curious and need your guidance to keep them out of harm's way.

Demonstrate just how much you love your dog by enrolling in a pet first-aid class. Contact your local humane society or ASPCA shelter for a class in your area.

Resist the temptation to share your sweet tooth with your dog by giving him some of your chocolate chip cookies and milk. Chocolate contains theobromine, a stimulant related to caffeine that can create a dangerous reaction in your dog.

ASSEMBLE A FIRST-AID KIT

Invest in a first-aid kit for your dog. A well-stocked kit should contain:
- Cold packs
- Nonstick sterile gauze pads
- Lightweight adhesive tape that won't stick to wounds
- Cotton balls
- Cotton-tipped ear swabs
- Antiseptic wipes
- Tweezers
- Antibiotic ointment
- Diphenhydramine (Benadryl) for bites and stings
- Coated buffered aspirin (*Note:* Never give acetaminophen or ibuprofen)
- Phone numbers of your veterinarian and emergency pet clinic

Carob is a much safer sweet treat. As for milk, shy away from serving it, especially to puppies. Their immature digestive systems cannot always properly break down the ingredients.

Provide your dog with an expandable collar so it doesn't cut into his skin as he grows. Use harnesses instead of collars for small-necked dogs.

Memorize this number: (900) 680-0000. It's the hot line for the National Animal Poison Control Center. You will be billed $45 per case, directly to your phone number, and there is no time limit. Or dial (888) 426-4435 to charge the fee to a major credit card. Whichever phone option you choose, rest assured that this hot line is open 24 hours a day, seven days a week. When you call, provide the name and amount of the poison your animal was exposed to; how long ago the exposure occurred; the species, breed, age, sex, and weight of your pet; and the symptoms she is displaying. Poisoning signs include listlessness, abdominal pain, vomiting, diarrhea, muscle tremors, lack of coordination, and fever.

Call (888) PETS-911 (888-738-7911) — toll free — to contact the national pet emergency hot line, which is staffed by trained professionals. They will put you in touch with a pet clinic in your area if your dog needs emergency care or becomes lost.

Keep poisonous houseplants safely out of your dog's reach by hanging them on ceiling hooks. Dogs can get sick, even die, if they eat these plants: azalea, daffodil bulbs, dieffenbachia, geraniums, holly, impatiens, ivy, mistletoe, morning glory, oleander, philodendron, and poinsettia. For a complete list, check the Web site of the Humane Society of the United States at www.hsus.org

Elevate your shampoo, conditioner, soap, and razor out of paw and nose reach in your shower.

Keep the lid down to prevent your dog from using the toilet as an auxiliary drinking bowl. The water may look clean, but it can harbor disease-causing bacteria.

Use safety electrical cords that prevent shocks or sparks if gnawed on. Dust electrical cords with cayenne pepper or Bitter Apple spray (available at pet stores) to discourage chewing.

Wipe up and flush away any automotive spills immediately. Keep your dogs indoors when you are changing antifreeze. Bring used antifreeze to recycling centers for proper disposal. Make sure your car has no coolant leaks.

Store cleaning supplies and other doggie hazards inside cabinets with childproof latches.

Don't use antifreeze that contains ethylene glycol (EG) — the sweet taste is attractive, but just 2 ounces can kill a dog. It may drip from a leaky hose or radiator or be spilled during coolant changes. Once swallowed, EG rapidly crystallizes and attacks the kidneys. If you suspect your dog has ingested toxic antifreeze, call the vet immediately; there are no symptoms at first. Avoid this situation by switching to antifreeze that contains pylene glycol (PG). PG performs just as well as conventional antifreeze against freezing, overheating, and corrosion, and it is essentially nontoxic to pets. It is also environmentally friendly, since it's biodegradable and contains no phosphates.

Quit smoking. Secondhand smoke bothers dogs, too. In fact, one in five dogs suffers from some type of allergy, including smoke allergy.

He who learns fast, gets fewer treats.

— **Moose**

24

Smooth Moves

We're a highly mobile society. Job changes, marriages, and other events cause us to pack up and move elsewhere. Days, even weeks before you pack the first box, your dog already senses the impending change.

Moving On

Moving is a stressful time for you, but don't overlook the nervousness in your dog. Now more than ever she needs your reassurance that everything will be fine. During a quiet moment, tell her about the big move. Let her know that she is coming with you and that the new place offers new sights and smells. She may not understand your words, but she will understand your excitement and loyalty.

Confine your dog to one room or a fenced backyard while the movers trek in and out. Provide one of your recently worn T-shirts and a favorite toy for comfort. Check on the dog often.

Contact the local humane society for a list of pet-friendly landlords in your area.

Present your dog's Canine Good Citizen certification. This program teaches dogs manners and how to act in safe ways. Dogs must pass 10 areas before earning this distinction. For information, contact the American Kennel Club at (919) 233-9767 or on the Web at www.akc.org.

When searching for a new place, create a sensational résumé for your dog that highlights his terrific traits. Indicate that he is up-to-date on all vet visits, and include letters of reference from your vet, current landlord, and neighbors. Provide documentation that your dog aced obedience class.

Try to re-create your dog's special spot in your new house to help him feel more at home. Place your sweatshirt in his bed so he can savor the smell.

25

Take a Walk on the Wag Side

Dogs live for walks. Some dogs are even savvy enough to put the leash in their mouth and deliver it to you.

A Walk in the Park

Provide soft, cushy walks for your dog by sticking to grass and dirt and avoiding hard, hot surfaces, such as asphalt, whenever possible.

Take your dog to a dog park or another place where he can make doggie friends. Make sure both dogs are on leashes during the introduction. If your dog makes a friend, exchange phone numbers with the friend's owner so you can rendezvous.

THE JOY OF JOGGING

You'll not find a more reliable running mate than your dog. He won't brush you off because he partied too late the night before or because his sneakers are too damp. To pamper your canine jogger and keep him in great shape:

- Check with the vet to make sure your dog is up to the challenge.
- Use a leather leash. It's easier to grip and won't cut into your hand like nylon can.
- Guide your dog by extending your leg to the side each time she tries to cut in front of you.
- For jogs longer than 20 minutes, put a lightweight pack on your dog to hold her water supply. Stash a few plastic bags to scoop up any poop.
- Run on grass whenever possible to cushion your dog's pads.
- Time your runs for early morning or midevening — never during the heat of the day.
- Check your dog's paws for any signs of cuts or injuries after each jog.
- Put safety lights and reflective tape on both of you for nighttime jaunts.
- Treat joint pain with moist heat after a run. Dampen a towel, wring it out, and stick it in the microwave oven for 45 seconds. Place it on your dog's sore joint for 5 to 10 minutes.

26

Games Dogs Play

Organized play is a real dog pleaser. It keeps your dog's mind off worries and promotes healthy sleep, relaxation, and contentment. Dogs that exercise regularly are less likely to develop behavioral problems, as well.

Helpful Hints

Here are some basic tips for your playtimes together:

- 🐾 Schedule exercise before meals, not immediately after. This prevents stomachaches and muscle cramps.

- 🐾 Gradually build up the duration and intensity of the exercise activity. Don't expect your dog to chase a Frisbee for 2 hours on his first introduction to this sport.
- 🐾 Treat your dog to warm-ups and cool-downs with gentle, stretching massages.
- 🐾 Never force your dog to do an activity she doesn't like.
- 🐾 Always provide a ready supply of water.
- 🐾 Stop the activity if your dog sits down in the middle of it. He may be fatigued.

Take It Outside

Frisbee fetching. Your dog may be a natural at this sport. Find out by first engaging him in a friendly game of fetch with a small fabric-covered disk. Toss the disk into the air and note whenever your dog follows it with his eyes — that's a very good sign. Praise and repeat. Once he can chase, catch, and return the disk consistently, switch to the traditional hard plastic Frisbee.

Tennis ball retrieval. When you want to practice your tennis serves and no one is available, bring your dog to the enclosed courts (if dogs are allowed). You get your exercise with your lobs and slams while your dog gets a workout fetching and retrieving the tennis balls.

Agility training. This popular sport is like the decathlon for dogs. Agility competitions are contested on timed obstacle courses featuring teeter-totters, steep inclines, tires to leap through, poles to weave around, snakelike tunnels, and narrow beams to walk on. Mutts and pedigrees are on equal footing in this sport. Dogs must pay attention to hand commands, eye contact, and clapping to navigate successfully. For more details, contact the United States Dog Agility Association in Dallas, TX at (972) 231-9700 or on the Web at www.usdaa.com.

Flyball. This is a relay race for ball-crazy dogs. The goal is to leap over four hurdles, hit a box to release a ball into the air, snag the ball, and race back to the starting line. Herding and retrieving breeds really love this sport.

27

Take the Fright Out of Vet Visits

If you've just moved or your old vet has relocated, a trip to the new vet can be just as scary for you as it is for your dog. Word of mouth is a terrific way to locate a compassionate and skillful veterinarian. Talk with pet-owning neighbors, friends, and co-workers for recommendations.

What else can you do to ensure that you find the best vet for you *and* your furry friend?

Getting to Know You

Contact the American Animal Hospital Association (AAHA) in Denver, Colorado. This professional organization of licensed vets promotes standards for pet care. Call AAHA's toll free number, (800) 252-2242, or tap into www.aahanet.org for assistance.

If possible, tour the veterinary clinic before booking your first appointment. High-quality clinics will gladly guide you through their facilities and answer your questions. Look for cleanliness in the waiting room, exam rooms, labs, and kennel areas. Find out whether the clinic has evening and weekend hours and accommodates after-hours emergencies. Ask about continuing education classes for staff as well as specialties they may have.

Treat your dog to a practice run when introducing her to a new dog doc. Bring your dog into the clinic and let her investigate. Have the vet and his staff give healthy treats to your dog so that she associates the clinic and staff with good thoughts. Then schedule an appointment for an official physical exam. And don't forget to pack the treats!

Have your veterinarian perform yearly blood, urine, and other lab tests on dogs over age five to detect early signs of disease or other problems.

28

Avoid creating a Chow Hound

Sure, we like to indulge our doggie pals with foods, but we're slowly killing them with kindness. Show true love by not overfeeding your dog. Each extra ounce of body fat reduces your dog's longevity, mobility, and vitality.

Improve Your Monitoring Skills

Is your dog too chubby? Place both thumbs on your dog's backbone. Rub your fingers along his rib cage. If you can't feel the rib cage through the furry flap, he's probably overweight.

Weigh your dog once a week using the same scale. Record the weight to the exact ounce on a notepad near her food containers. A weight gain of a couple of pounds on an adult dog over a month's time is your signal to cut back on the chow and step up the exercise time. Two extra pounds on a dog is like 10 to 20 pounds in a person.

For your overweight dog, gradually reduce the amount of chow by 10 percent or so weekly.

Help your pudgy pooch lose a few pounds by adding more dietary fiber to her meals. Fiber not only improves digestion but also helps lessen the chance of constipation.

Sprinkle a teaspoon of kelp powder on your dog's food. Or try 1 capsule of lecithin (open it first) or 1 teaspoon of organic apple cider vinegar in his water bowl. All three help speed the dog's metabolism and break down fats.

Limit your dog to a 20-minute mealtime. Remove his dish. If there are any leftovers, you're feeding him too much. Slightly reduce the portion.

29

A Backyard Fit for a Dog

Although your dog should spend most of his days and all of his nights inside with you, every dog deserves his very own "guesthouse" in your backyard. A doghouse will keep him warm and dry and will provide necessary shade on warmer days.

In the Doghouse

When creating or selecting a doghouse, factor in these pooch amenities:

- Make sure the floor is at least 4 inches off the ground and well insulated.

- Give the doghouse four wheels so you can easily relocate it as needed.
- Build a slanted roof so snow and rain won't pile up on top.
- Select a design with a hinged roof so that you can lift it and clean inside easily.
- Mist flea and tick spray inside the doghouse once a week, especially during humid summer months.
- Strew straw or cedar shavings on the floor. Don't use newspapers (the ink can discolor fur and cause allergic reactions) or hay (it tends to get moldy and can cause a fungal infection).
- Size the doghouse so that your dog can turn around in it and can stretch out without touching the sides or poking out the front opening.
- Make sure the house is amply ventilated.
- Skip mansion-sized doghouses. Dogs rely on their body heat inside confined spaces to keep from shivering on cold days.
- Situate the entrance away from the prevailing winds.
- Fasten a thick, clear plastic flap on the front entrance that allows for easy ins and outs while also keeping out flying insects, rain, sleet, and snow.
- Use nontoxic paint only; dogs are prone to chewing.
- Turn an ordinary doghouse into a heated and air-conditioned haven by connecting it to your own house's heater and air conditioner, but monitor the temperature closely.

30

Cruising With Your Canine

If the only time your dog rides in the car is to visit the veterinarian, it's no wonder he begins to whimper and hide under the bed the minute you jingle your car keys. Ninety-nine percent of car rides should be fun for your dog. You may not be able to make him beg to go for a checkup, but here are some handy tips to guarantee that your road trips leave your dog howling with happiness.

Rover's Road Trip

Hold off on feeding your dog for a few hours prior to the start of your trip. No need to raise the risk of a stomachache caused by motion sickness.

Work your way up to longer trips by first getting your dog used to frequent short trips. Start by taking him to dog-pleasing places: dog parks, the beach, Grandma's house, or the biscuit-delivering teller at your drive-through bank window. Soon, your dog will forget about the vet and start to associate good events with the car. Short trips also help you determine how your dog reacts inside a car and if he is prone to motion sickness.

Never leave your dog inside the car — at any time of year, but especially in the hot summer — even for a few minutes. Leaving the windows open a crack is no guarantee against heatstroke. Your dog can become severely sick, or even die.

Give your dog a flea bath before making a long trip. Neither one of you would like to be itchy and scratching on the interstate.

Keep a stash of healthy road treats tucked inside the glove compartment or a small cooler. When you make a food stop at a drive-through window, treat your dog to nutritious biscuits, carrot sticks, celery stalks, or apple slices.

Resist the temptation to buy your dog a burger. Instead give her a very small piece of meat, or better yet, just let her lick your greasy fingers after you're done. Fat is very hard for dogs to digest, putting your dog at risk for pancreatitis, not to mention obesity and all the problems that go with it, such as diabetes and liver and heart disease.

Buckle up your beagle — and every other dog. An unrestrained 60-pound dog in a 30-mph crash can generate an impact force against the windshield, seat back, or another passenger of 1,200 pounds! Use a harness with a dog seat belt, or keep your dog in a crate. Either option ensures a safer ride for your dog, say folks from the Humane Society of the United States. Certain models of Saab, Audi, and Subaru recognize the joy of canine companionship and have dog restraint safety systems. Some also offer travel bowls, gear bars, water bottles, a folding car bed, and an air purifier to pamper your cruising canine.

Attach a leash to your dog before letting her out of the car to prevent escapes or accidents.

Carry water and a bowl for your dog, even on short rides. A quick trip can sometimes unexpectedly become a long journey.

Keep a spray bottle of water within reach. On long, hot rides, spritz your dog's face and paws for a real cool-down.

Pack all-natural springwater in plastic, resealable containers. Springwater contains no additives or preservatives, making it a lip-smacking beverage of choice for your thirsty canine. Bottled water is purer than tap water, which may contain chlorine, lead, and disease-causing contaminants.

Resist the temptation to let your dog stick her face out the car window. Flying debris can easily injure her eyes. Crack the window only enough to keep the air flowing. If your dog insists on poking her head out the window, strap on some safety goggles. She'll truly look the part of copilot!

Excessive drooling is a sure sign that your dog is beginning to suffer car sickness. Park at a safe place and walk him for 5 or 10 minutes.

Skip the boring talk radio shows and flip to an oldies station. Serenade your dog with classic tunes from the '60s, '70s, and '80s. Who knows? She may be inspired to become your howling backup singer!

Every two or three hours, stop at safe places for potty breaks and to stretch.

Place favorite chew toys and a blanket inside your dog's crate for comfort.

TRAVEL SAFETY TIP

Consider having your veterinarian insert an identification microchip under your dog's skin, usually on the back of the neck. Many animal shelters and veterinary clinics have scanners that can be run over the dog's back to reveal your name, contact information, and pet's name, should she get lost.

31

Splish, Splash — Fido's Taking a Bath

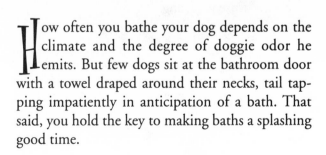

How often you bathe your dog depends on the climate and the degree of doggie odor he emits. But few dogs sit at the bathroom door with a towel draped around their necks, tail tapping impatiently in anticipation of a bath. That said, you hold the key to making baths a splashing good time.

Tub Fun

Don't wash your dog more than two or three times a week; cleaning chemicals can damage sensitive skin.

Dress to get wet. Slip into your bathing suit or don a rubberized apron. Believe me, sooner or later you'll get the full force of a full-body shake.

Size up your dog. For dogs under 15 pounds, kitchen sinks are perfect bathtubs. They are at a great height for you, and you'll have a handy spray attachment available. Place a towel in the sink to keep your dog from slipping. Put other towels and cleaning supplies within easy reach. For flea infestation, don't worry; most kitchen sinks can be disinfected safely with bleach.

For medium-sized dogs, utility sinks or bathtubs are ideal. Install a spray attachment. Kneel to scrub and rinse your dog.

For large- to giant-sized dogs, go with a shower stall. Buy a hand-held spray attachment for the showerhead to make the job faster and easier.

Put cotton balls in your dog's ears to keep water from entering his ear canals.

Customize the bathtub for medium dogs and the shower stall for large dogs with rubber, no-slip mats on their floors. Have cotton balls, eye ointment, shampoo, a bucket for diluting shampoo, a sponge for scrubbing, and plenty of drying towels within easy reach.

Never bathe your dog outdoors when the temperature is below 65°F. Outdoor faucets are usually designed to deliver only cold water.

Invest in a grooming noose that attaches to the sink or tub with a rubber suction cup. The noose slips over your dog's head and fastens to the suction cup. It's a safety device that prevents your slippery wet dog from leaping out of the tub or sink and possibly injuring herself.

Always speak to your dog in friendly, upbeat, reassuring tones from start to finish. Let him know what you're planning to do each step of the way. He may not understand your words, but your meaning will come across loud and clear.

Your dog's gotta shake. Once you've rinsed off the soap, swathe her in two towels. Let those two towels soak up most of the water. Then close the curtain or shower stall door and let her shake. Finish with a third dry towel.

Try putting two drops of shampoo in a large jug and filling it with warm water. Pour the jug of soapy water over the dog's coat before you begin wetting her down. This permits water to penetrate your dog's natural oil coating faster. Then work the shampoo evenly into his coat with your fingertips, not your finernails.

Install a showerhead with a hose that can bend and stretch easily.

Once your dog is wet with warm water, work in the soap from one end to the other, starting at the head. Rinse in the same order. Rinse a second time to wash soap out of the folds of skin.

Unless your dog has a skin condition that requires a special medicated shampoo, use baby shampoo or pet shampoo. Skip conditioners created for people; these products leave dog skin greasy.

HELP! MY DOG STINKS!

When you can't bathe your stinky dog, take away the pungent smell by sprinkling some baking soda on his coat. Use your fingers to work it into the fur. Baking soda is like nature's perfume, and it absorbs odors.

32

Hiking, Biking & Swimming

Bring out the adventurous soul in your dog by treating him to a rustic hike, a vigorous bike ride, or a cooling swim. Athletic dogs love to be our workout partners. But before you and your dog tackle these highly physical activities, make sure you're both fit. Get a physical from your physician and a thorough exam from the vet.

Fitness Tips

Build up both of your endurance levels gradually over several weeks.

Bring plenty of water. Dogs, on average, need about 12 ounces of water before *and* after hiking. During the trek, give your dog 12 ounces of water every 30 minutes to keep him hydrated. Carry a doggie canteen that doubles as a water and food dish or rely on a collapsible nylon dish.

Consider bringing a portable water purifier or a supply of iodine-based tablets that filter out harmful bacteria for times when you can't get to a clean water source.

Plan on lots of rest stops. Let your dog rest his paws every 30 minutes or so.

Make the pool welcoming by bringing one of your dog's floating toys into the water with you.

Do you have a dog that just loves to join you on your bike rides? Only bike with a dog trained — and willing — to keep pace with you by running to your left and never in front of you. Also, be sure that your cycling skills are up to par; neither of you needs a head-over-handlebars spill. Some companies make devices that fit low on the frame or rear wheel so that you can attach a leash. Look for products with coil springs that absorb and reduce the effects of sudden jerks and pulls so that you can keep both hands on the handlebars and maintain your balance. Also make sure the device features a safety release that quickly frees your dog should she head for the wrong side of a tree, hydrant, pole, or other obstacle.

Swimming is a great exercise because it doesn't put weight and stress on the joints. If you want to see whether your dog likes to swim, wrap his torso in a soft vinyl foam life preserver made for dogs.

Help your dog get her sea legs by placing a large potted plant or concrete figurine near the pool steps to mark the exit. Always encourage your dog to swim toward the steps. Reward her when she does.

To teach your dog to swim, hold him securely under his chest. Slowly bring him into water just deep enough so that his feet don't touch bottom. Guide him toward the water's edge and gradually let go. Chaperone him as he swims.

Bring a canine life preserver for canoe and boat rides. Dogs can become injured jumping out of a boat or can become tired swimming a long distance to shore.

Thoroughly dry your dog's ears after swimming to prevent ear infections.

33

Doggie Day Care

Doggie day care offers a guilt-free solution for on-the-go dog owners, since these facilities provide plenty of socialization for your dog. But how do you decide which facility is best?

Making Your Selection

Keep these points in mind when searching for just the right place for your pooch:

- 🐾 Tour the day care center before leaving your dog there.
- 🐾 Check to see that the center's play area is clean, odor free, safe, comfortable, and well ventilated.

- 🐾 Make sure that there are safe, enclosed outdoor areas for your dog.
- 🐾 Be sure that there are plenty of toys, beds, and supplies.
- 🐾 The ratio of people to dogs should be 1:10 or lower.

Get complete information on group play, group size, nap times, individual attention, use of toys, climate control, how new dogs are introduced, and what happens when dogs misbehave, bark, are aggressive, or are out of control.

Some day care centers have truly gone to the dogs — the spoiled dogs, that is! Some offer pooch-pampering amenities, such as grooming, massage, tennis ball chasing, and agility training.

Some day care centers have gone high tech and allow you to monitor your dog on-line. With cameras, modems, and Web servers, you can log on to watch videos of your dog updated every 20 seconds. Now you're only a few keyboard taps apart!

34

Paw-ticulars on Hotel Lodging

Practice pet-iquette while traveling with your canine mate. Bring only house-trained dogs to a hotel, and don't attempt to sneak your dog in. There are many reasons for the pet ban at certain hotels, including the welfare of guests who have pet allergies.

Traveling in Style

Be sure to pack your dog's favorite blanket or bedding to make her feel more at home in an otherwise strange place.

Always give your dog a good walk before you check in to prevent any accidental puddles.

Never leave your dog alone in the hotel room. He may become nervous in the strange surroundings and bark, chew, or dig holes in the carpet.

Tip the housekeeper well; there will be a little extra work involved in de-dogging the room after you depart.

Got a mouse? No, not the varmint type — the computer type! Click on to www.dogfriendly.com for a free listing of pet-friendly hotels and attractions for you and your dog.

Therefore to this dog will I,
Tenderly not scornfully,
Render praise and favor.

    — Elizabeth Barrett Browning

35

Bone Appetite

Most dogs will eat anything they can get their paws on. Give them healthy choices beyond commercial dog food. Keep these foods on hand for homemade meals: lean ground beef or turkey, cooked beef liver, brown rice, bran, bonemeal, corn oil, iodized salt, low-fat cottage cheese, carrots, scrambled eggs, cauliflower, calcium phosphate, garlic powder, cloves, and potatoes. Try the following recipes for meals that will delight your dog — and make you feel great for making them.

Dog Biscuits Baked with Love

Here's a popular recipe shared by many dog lovers.

1 cup cornmeal
Pinch of salt
2 cups unbleached wheat flour
1 egg
3 tablespoons vegetable oil
2 teaspoons chopped parsley
¾ cup chicken broth

1. Preheat the oven to 400°F.

2. Mix the cornmeal, salt, and flour in one bowl.

3. In a separate and larger bowl, whip the egg with the vegetable oil, chopped parsley, and chicken broth. Add the flour mixture and mix until a soft dough forms.

4. Knead the dough and roll it out to half-inch thickness. Use cookie cutters to cut the dough into canine-pleasing shapes, such as fire hydrants, bones, cars, and cats.

5. Bake for 15 minutes. Cool the biscuits before serving.

TLC Leftovers

This tasty recipe will feed a medium-sized dog.

4 ounces lean ground beef
4 ounces low-fat or fat-free cottage cheese
1 cup grated or cooked carrots
1 cup cooked and chopped green beans
1 teaspoon bonemeal powder

1. Cook the ground beef in a pan. Drain off the fat and allow the meat to cool.

2. Add the remaining ingredients and mix well. Serve as a Sunday treat.

Doggone Goodness

Treat your dog to a home-cooked meal that is healthy and delicious. Surprise him on his birthday, for finishing dog obedience training, or for learning a new trick. Here's a favorite recipe that my grandma taught me to make for Crackers, our beagle.

    1   cup raw rolled oats
    3   eggs baked in the oven for 10 minutes at 350°F
    1   teaspoon calcium powder
    1   teaspoon magnesium powder
    1   teaspoon bonemeal powder
    ½   cup cottage cheese (small curd)
    1   cup raw carrots (diced or grated)
    ½   cup raw chopped or ground turkey
        Brewer's yeast (optional)

1. Bring 2 cups of water to a boil on the stovetop. Add the raw oats, cover with a lid, reduce to medium heat, and cook for 3 minutes.

2. Turn off the heat and let the pan stand for another 10 minutes, then add the rest of the ingredients.

3. Spoon the mixture into your dog's bowl. As an added treat, sprinkle some brewer's yeast on top.

36

Holy Hounds

Yes, we're well aware that God spelled backward is Dog. Our canine friends possess a strong sense of spirituality that we are just beginning to understand. But, fortunately, more folks are starting to recognize the spiritual bond that they have with their dogs.

Praying with Your Pooch

Arrange a private benediction ceremony for your dog with your friends and neighbors.

Mark your calendar for the first week of October and plan ahead. During that week, you can have your dog blessed by a priest at Washington National Cathedral in the nation's capital.

Head to the Big Apple. The Blessing of the Animals is performed every Christmas Eve at the Central Presbyterian Church on Park Avenue and 64th Street in New York City.

If Washington, D.C. and New York City are too far away, check your local newspaper listings or contact your local humane society to find out details on pet blessings in your area. They are usually scheduled around Christmas or the Feast Day of St. Francis of Assisi (October 4).

Practice what you've been preached. Work with your local animal shelters to bring adoptable dogs to your church or synagogue after worship service for adoption.

Pray with your dog, offering sincere gratitude for being blessed with such a loving pal. Create a time each day for quiet, calm reflection.

Get in the habit of saying grace with your pet at mealtimes, or give thanks as you cuddle him.

37

Good Toys, Bad Toys

When it comes to pet toys, use the same precaution you do with small children: Keep toys with removable parts out of your dog's way. Squeaky toys or stuffed animals with plastic eyes can pose choking hazards for a dog who treats his mouth like a catcher's mitt.

Choose Wisely

For a fun round of fetch, use only balls that bounce well.

Select durable toys that can pass the chew test. Toys made of hard rubber or nylon are better than soft foam balls that can be easily shredded into small pieces.

Rawhide doggie chews may be contaminated with salmonella, which can infect your dog. Rinse them in hot water and keep them away from heat, which encourages bacteria growth. They can also pose a choking hazard. Give them to your dog only when you're supervising him.

Toys for your dog should be fun, interactive, and brightly colored.

Choose toys made of strong, safe materials. Topping the list are vinyl, latex, nylon, and simulated lambskin.

Don't use knotted socks or old shoes. It will only teach your puppy or dog that it's okay to chew on all socks and shoes.

Provide hollow toys filled with treats; these keep your dog mentally and physically busy. Stuff the toys with peanut butter, cream cheese, or kibble.

climatize Your Canine

You may not be able to put a leash on Mother Nature or teach her to heel, but you can buffer your pooch from extreme temperatures. Protection is especially important for very young and very old dogs.

Summertime Safety

During the dog days of summer when the sun is bright and humidity seems to drip from trees, keep your dog cool by following these tips.

Schedule your walks for early morning and evening, when the sun is not so menacing. If you need to walk your dog in the middle of the day during the summer, stick to grassy areas and stay away from the searing asphalt.

Fit your four-legged pal with doggie booties to prevent his paw pads from sizzling on the hot pavement.

Apply a little sunscreen around the eyes, ears, nose, and underbellies of light-colored dogs. They are most at risk for sunburn.

Designate a plastic kiddie pool in your yard as your dog's personal water wonderland.

Recognize that black and dark brown dogs are more prone to heat exhaustion than white or light-colored dogs. Give them plenty of water and extra shade.

Go easy on exercise if your dog has a short, pushed-in face. These dogs have more difficulty breathing in hot, humid weather.

Wintertime Wariness

When the weather is frightfully cold, keep your dog warm and help him dodge hypothermia by following these helpful hints.

Keep a doggie rain slicker (with hood) within easy reach of the door to shelter your dog during those gotta-go-outside-in-the-rain potty breaks.

After a brisk walk, wrap your dog's torso in warm towels just pulled from the dryer

Time your dog's outdoor exposure on the basis of the thickness of her winter coat, her age, and her weight. A senior dog barely tipping the scales at 10 pounds shouldn't be out for more than 10 minutes when the thermometer reads 25°F or less. A healthy adult dog sporting a thick winter coat can tolerate a 20-minute walk in 25°F weather. Thin-coated small dogs need doggie coats before venturing outside if the weather is 40°F or below.

Wash your dog's paws of chemical salts thrown on sidewalks to melt ice. These can irritate footpads and can be poisonous if the dog licks her paws.

Stop static electricity by keeping your house at 50 percent humidity during the winter months.

39

Dog Park Etiquette

With all the strict municipal leash laws, you may think it's impossible to ever find a place to let your dog run unleashed at full stride. Good news: The number of dog parks springing up around the country stands at 600 and counting. These parks allow dogs to run and play in a safe and inviting environment. Check out the Web site www.dogpark.com for a list of dog-friendly places in your area.

Mind Your Manners

Of course, certain rules apply to make the dog park a fun — and safe — place for all. Among some common rules are the following principles.

Make sure your dog has up-to-date vaccinations, is healthy, and is wearing identification tags.

Leave puppies at home until they've had all their puppy shots and have demonstrated the ability to obey "sit," "stay," and "come" commands.

Keep an eye on your dog at all times and never detach the leash until you've reached the designated off-leash area.

Bring water (most places provide drinking fountains at dog-eye levels) but leave food in your car. This is a playground for dogs — not a picnic area.

Keep aggressive dogs leashed — or better yet, leave them at home to avoid a dog fight.

Bring your pooper-scooper and plastic bags just in case the park doesn't provide them.

Never bring more dogs from your household than you can control. The maximum is three or four, depending on how well behaved they are and how well they stick together.

40

Lend a Paw

If you adopted a puppy or dog from an animal shelter, that's paws-itively great! But don't make that your last visit to a shelter. Help homeless dogs by making their shelter stays more pleasant. Each shelter has different needs and programs; ask what services are needed most.

You *Can* Help

Even if you don't have a lot of time to give, consider any of these acts of kindness.

Volunteer as a dog walker once a week on your lunch hour. Take the opportunity to let a caged dog stretch his legs and breathe outdoor smells.

Offer to be an animal socializer at a shelter. The goal is to have volunteers play with dogs in a setting resembling a living room to get them used to household furnishings and being handled.

Agree to be a volunteer adoption counselor. Help create a long-lasting union by pairing people with appropriate dogs.

BUT I HAVE NO TIME TO SPARE!

If you're really taxed for time, open your wallet and pamper shelter dogs in these ways:
- Donate new collars, leashes, food, and water bowls.
- Provide comfy blankets or doggie beds.
- Take your weekly movie money and spend it at a pet store on toys and treats for shelter dogs. This act is rated PG — Pure Goodness!

Become a dog foster parent and provide a temporary loving home for sheltered puppies or dogs to build up their socialization skills. Once they leave your home, their chances of being adopted should soar!

41

Legal Beagles

Where there's a will, there's a way of life for your dog . . . long after you're gone. Don't run the risk of your best buddy not having a place to go in the event of your death.

In You They Trust

Establish a pet trust that designates someone to care for your faithful dog and provides the finances for his lifelong care after you die. You can designate a specific amount to be spent monthly or annually for your dog or just leave it up to the executor's discretion. You can also specify that any unused balance of the trust money be donated to a humane society, animal shelter, or favorite animal charity. Legal trusts can cost from $75 to $400 to set up.

The Humane Society of the United States offers a free brochure, "Planning for Your Pet's Future Without You." It outlines steps to take to prepare for the unexpected and to ensure that your dog will be cared for in a safe, loving environment after you die. Obtain the brochure by calling the HSUS at (202) 452-1100 or writing them at HSUS, Planned Giving Department, 2100 L Street NW, Washington, D.C. 20037.

If your dear old, ailing Aunt Nila passed away and left a sweet-hearted dog behind, consider pairing him with another ailing or elderly person. Check with your local humane society or local chapter of the American Association of Retired Persons to try to place the dog in a new home. Dogs that have lived with people in poor health are blessed with the temperament to help another such person.

Besides creating a will, you need to take steps to keep your dog a law-abiding canine citizen. Check with your local health department about licensing rules in your community. There may be particular laws on leash usage, the wearing of identification tags, and housing restrictions. Follow the law to make life easier for your dog.

42

Doggie Karma

I'm not talking about doggie voodoo. But, like you, your dog is a spiritual being. In fact, some animal experts are convinced that dogs have psychic powers that we're only just beginning to understand and study. How else can we explain lost dogs who travel thousands of miles and find their way home, or dogs able to predict epileptic seizures in people minutes before they occur?

Keep in Touch

Talk to a pet psychic to learn how your dearly departed is doing in doggie heaven. He may offer you words of advice from the great beyond. Arrange for a few friends to bring pictures of their late but great pooches to a group session with a pet psychic. You can find pet psychics in the phonebook or on the Internet.

Contact a pet psychic or pet communicator to help you find out what your dog likes and dislikes and how you can improve his home life. Take the time to really tune in to your pet's psyche. Maybe he's jealous of the family cat, or hates chicken meat, or wants you to keep the Animal Planet channel permanently on the television.

Meditate together. Pick a time when your dog is quiet, such as after a nap or a meal. Go to a quiet room (turn off the phone and television), and have your dog sit or lie next to you. Close your eyes and silently think of happy memories you share with your dog. Clear your head of other distractions and focus only on your relationship with your dog. Start with 5 minutes and gradually work up to 20 minutes at a time, but don't force your dog to fit your schedule.

43

Protect With Pet Insurance

Monthly household budgets often overlook a major potential drain on the family income: medical costs for our favorite canine chums.

Only 1 percent of American pet owners has pet health insurance; that's a striking contrast to the more than 50 percent of Swedish dog owners. No one wants to risk "economic euthanasia." Dogs should be put down only when it is medically necessary to relieve them of pain and suffering and not because medical care is too costly.

Why Bother with Insurance?

If your dog develops a chronic medical condition, you could be faced with some large bills. For instance, the average cost of a kidney transplant for a dog is $7,000. Hip replacements can run $2,500 and higher. Certain types of cancer treatment can cost as much as $10,000. Are you prepared to handle such costs?

Pet health insurance, in the long run, is a money-saving way to ensure that your dog's medical needs will always be met. Premiums vary among companies as well as among dogs. Typically, premiums are less expensive for puppies and healthy adult dogs than for senior dogs and those with diagnosed conditions, such as allergies or cancer.

In most cases, insurance will cover 70 to 90 percent of your dog's medical expenses. Veterinary Pet Insurance, based in Anaheim, California, is the nation's largest pet health insurer. Their health plans cover office visits, prescriptions, treatment, lab fees, X rays, surgery, and chiropractic procedures performed by a licensed veterinarian. You pay the bill in full, file a claim with VPI, and get reimbursed within 7 to 10 working days. The policy permits you to take your insured pet to any licensed veterinarian, veterinary specialist, or animal hospital worldwide. For more details, contact VPI at (800) USA-PETS (872-7387) or through its Web site at www.petinsurance.com.

44

Picking a Pet-Pleasing Sitter

Ideally, you should have the pet sitter stop by a few times and visit with your dog before you go away on a trip. This strategy helps your dog feel more comfortable with the pet sitter and reduces his anxiety level while you're gone. For local referrals, contact the National Association of Professional Pet Sitters (NAPPS) at (800) 296-PETS or its Web site at www.petsitters.org. Or call Pet Sitters International (PSI) at (800) 268-SITS or visit their Web site at www.petsit.com.

Tips for a Safe and Happy Visit

Make your refrigerator door "Dog Information Central." Post a note that lists your dog's name (and nickname), how much food she eats and when she eats it, location of the food, location of and directions for any medications, likes and dislikes, house rules, leash location, and most important, how to contact you and your vet.

CONSIDER THE EXTRAS

Ensure that your dog is safe and happy while you're away by providing the pet sitter with these essentials:

- Extra cash in case the food runs out
- Directions for setting the thermostat or air conditioning in case of dramatic changes in the weather
- The phone number of and directions to your regular veterinary clinic or hospital
- A list outlining potential pitfalls around the house (such as, "Always close all doors very quickly because Buttons likes to try to dart outside," or "Keep the toilet lid down because Frankie is a bowl drinker.")
- An introduction to a friendly neighbor before your departure (have them exchange phone numbers)

45

Home Alone

When you're away from home, don't expect your dog to fight boredom or anxiety by working a crossword puzzle, taking up cross-stitching, or writing the Great American Novel. Dogs think and act differently from people.

Low-Stress Partings

Does it seem like your dog wraps his front paws around your calf each time you try to leave the house? Or races to the front door and body slams you from excitement upon your return? Sounds like your dog has a case of separation anxiety. Show him how much you care for his welfare by following this advice.

Don't make a big deal about exiting or entering. Sadly, we're to blame for why some dogs make such a fuss to bid us bye-bye or hug us hello. We're flattered by the shower of attention. To break your dog's habit of leaping on you when you come in, ignore your dog for a few minutes. Or reach for a toy stashed in a basket by the door. Throw one as soon as you step inside. Your dog will learn to unleash his energy on the toy, not you.

Stage dress rehearsals. Spend 5 minutes sitting in a chair with your dog by your side. Don't talk to her or touch her. Do this to put her in a calm state. Then stand up, pick up your car keys, and walk outside out of sight for a minute or so. Reenter the house and again ignore your dog. Wait a few minutes before greeting her by name in a casual tone. Gradually build up to 10 to 15 minutes.

Confine your pet to one dog-proofed room or a crate until she learns to love chew toys and not your furniture or door frames.

Give your dog a job while you're gone. Stuff a hard rubber toy with his favorite food treat, such as peanut butter, kibble, cheese, or meat. He will spend hours trying to fish out those tasty morsels from the food-dispensing toy. By working the food out of a toy, your dog is engaged in scavenging and hunting activities and is less apt to tear up your couch out of boredom or nervousness.

Telephone your home twice a day and leave a friendly message for your dog on the answering machine. Sample: "Hey, Kosmo, how's my good dog doing? You're the number-one dog in the world. Be home soon." Make sure the volume is turned up high enough for your dog to hear it.

Leave your recently worn T-shirt in your dog's bed or at the foot of your bed to ease her anxiety.

Invite trusted neighbors or friends to stop by and play with your dog.

Scratch a dog and you'll find a permanent job.

—Franklin P. Jones

46

Cele-bark the Holidays

Dogs don't know the true meaning of Christmas or Hanukkah or Kwanza. They can't fathom why the neighborhood sounds like a battle zone during the Fourth of July, or why strange children wearing even stranger outfits are ringing the doorbell on Halloween and begging for — and receiving! — treats.

Holidays can be anxiety-filled times for our cherished canines. The best way to pamper your dog during these times of celebration is to protect him from harm and give him plenty of reassurance and TLC.

The Doggie Holiday Spirit

Don't force your dog to wear a bow around his neck during the 12 days of Christmas. He can trip or choke on these bows. A better option is to buy him a new collar in holiday colors at a fashion-conscious pet store.

Keep all cherished holiday ornaments, statues, and treasures out of the reach of wagging tails and nosey noses.

Wait a week or so after the holidays to adopt a puppy or add a new dog to your household. The holidays are stressful enough with all of their activities. Wait until you've gotten back into your regular routine before heading to the shelter.

Avoid edible decorations, such as popcorn or candy canes. A dog acting naughty rather than nice can suffer a stomach upset.

During Thanksgiving or other big food-feast holidays, don't share your special meal with your dog. Bones can choke animals. Rich gravy and pies can cause stomachaches. Instead, treat your dog with gourmet foods designed for dogs; this allows her to share the holiday bounty in a safer way.

Keep chocolate candy, chocolate chips, and baker's chocolate out of nose and paw reach. Chocolate is toxic to dogs and can cause vomiting and diarrhea, or even death.

Fill your dog's stocking with dog biscuits and chew toys or a brand new tennis ball.

Buy only nontoxic Christmas tree–water preservatives and artificial snow.

Keep your anxious dog in a quiet part of the house during holiday parties.

HAVE A HOUND HOLIDAY

Your dog may not be as thrilled about human holidays as you are. Instead of always expecting her to take part in your traditions, start a new tradition that you can enjoy together. Celebrate your dog's birthday by inviting over a few of her favorite four-legged friends. Serve some homemade dog biscuits, play games, or have the dogs show off their best tricks.

47

10 Canine Commandments

One way to make your dog happy and content is to give him a clear idea of your house rules. No need to act like Moses and shout these 10 commandments from the mountaintop. Instead, be consistent in your training and your dog will soon learn proper behavior.

Laying Down the Law

The way to a dog's happiness is through his stomach. Reinforce commands during training sessions with tiny pieces of treats. The small size is easy to chew and won't cause major weight gain. Limit your sessions to 20 minutes maximum; dogs have short attention spans by nature and need to shift their energies elsewhere. Most dogs will be free of stress once they:

- Know and obey the "stay" command. Tail wagging is tolerated but moving is not.
- Learn to sit. Dogs who master "sit" are less prone to pull you on walks, fight with other dogs, or jump on guests.
- Respect the "down" command.
- Come when you call them, even if it means abandoning a rabbit chase. Always follow "come" with praise once the dog returns to you.
- Accept the appeal of "heel." Dogs that walk on your left side are less apt to lunge or yank on the leash.
- Stand at attention on all four feet. This makes chores such as grooming and bathing faster and easier for both of you.
- Understand the "off" command. This instructs dogs to stop jumping on people or to vacate the furniture pronto.
- Strive to hear the magic word: "okay." This tells them that you are pleased and aware that they've behaved like angels.
- Obey the "drop it" command. It's a quick way to rescue your prized shoes from your dog's mouth.
- Recognize that the "bed" command means it's time to head for his sleeping place for nap or nightly snooze.

48

Super Supplements

Y ou can help your dog's muscles move more fluidly, put the shine back into his coat, and fend off itchy skin or achy joints. Although dog foods are constantly being fortified, dogs don't always get the right amount of vitamins and minerals that they need.

Make your dog her healthiest with supplements. Before you start, though, discuss the proper supplement dosages with a holistic veterinarian. You can locate one in your area by contacting the American Holistic Veterinary Medical Association at (410) 569-0795 or www.altvetmed.com.

What's the Best Choice for My Dog?

Here are some popular supplements that can keep your dog in optimal health.

Acidophilus. This beneficial bacteria helps detoxify and fortify the digestive tract as well as aid in the absorption of nutrients. Count on this supplement to treat diarrhea, gas, bad breath, and foul-smelling feces.

Amino acids. It may surprise you, but the biggest deficiency in dog diets is amino acids. If you remember back to your high school science class, these are the building blocks of protein that enhance hormone production, maintain healthy muscles and tissues, and support metabolism.

Antioxidants. To help you remember the most important antioxidants, think ACES. That stands for vitamins A, C, and E plus the mineral selenium. Antioxidants help fend off environmental toxins, lessen the risk for certain cancers, and bolster your dog's immune system.

Biotin. This multibenefit supplement aids in cellular growth, digestion, muscle formation, and skin repair.

Brewer's yeast. This is a natural source of quality protein, trace minerals, salts, and B vitamins. It also helps repel fleas.

B vitamins. This group, specifically biotin and folic acid, provide energy. These vitamins convert carbohydrates into glucose (blood sugar) and speed up metabolism. They also boost the immune system and produce healthy fur and skin.

Calcium, magnesium, phosphorus, and zinc. This foursome works together to keep your dog's nervous system working at its best. It also fortifies the teeth and bones. But be patient; it may be a month or so before you'll notice the results.

Cleansers and detoxifiers. Chlorophyll, algae, barley, wheatgrass, spinach, broccoli, and kelp bolster the immune system and cleanse the blood. These are ideal supplements for aging dogs and for those recovering from cancer or surgery.

Glucosamine and chondroitin sulfate. These supplements are effective in combating arthritis. They reduce joint swelling, improve circulation, and promote production of synovial fluid, which lubricates the joints. Shark cartilage tablets can also be taken daily to enhance joint mobility that has been limited by arthritis.

Iodine. This vital mineral helps dogs maintain a healthy weight, stimulates normal bone growth, and boosts energy levels.

Omega-6 and omega-3 fatty acid supplements. Tame itchy skin due to allergies by giving these supplements. They also assist cell development in the immune system and brain.

Papaya enzyme. Clear the air of doggie gas by feeding your flatulent four-legged friend this enzyme. It naturally breaks down gas-producing particles in the dog's digestive tract.

GIVING SUPPLEMENTS

Pamper your dog's health by following these supplement guidelines:
- Take into account your dog's size, age, physical condition, and stress level.
- Always follow label directions and never oversupplement.
- Introduce one supplement at a time to your dog's breakfast or dinner. Wait a few days to detect any side effects before adding another supplement.

49

'Net Surfin' With Your Dog

I've yet to see a dog operate a computer mouse and tap onto a Web site. That's where you need to enter the scene. The Internet has really been going to the dogs — in a good way. There are plenty of reputable sites that offer terrific tips and advice on how to be a truly great owner.

The Best of the Web

Here are some of my favorite Web sites that cater to the needs and wants of canines:

- 🐾 Healthypet, www.healthypet.com
- 🐾 Petsmart, www.petsmart.com
- 🐾 Petco, www.petco.com
- 🐾 Petopia, www.petopia.com
- 🐾 PetSource, www.petsource.com
- 🐾 The Pet Channel, www.thepetchannel.com
- 🐾 Acme Pet, www.acmepet.com

NUMBERS TO KEEP BY THE PHONE

- **Canine Resource and Referral Helpline,** sponsored by the American Dog Trainers Network — (212) 727-7257 (1–3 P.M. EST).
- **Lost and Found Hotline** — (900) 535-1515. For a minor per-minute fee, they'll help you if you've lost a pet. Call (800) 755-8111 toll free to report finding a pet.
- **PetFinders** — (800) 666-5678.
- **American Veterinary Medical Association** — (847) 925-8070.
- **American Humane Association** — (303) 792-9900.
- **Humane Society of the United States** — (202) 452-1100.
- **American Society for the Prevention of Cruelty to Animals** — (212) 876-7700.

50

Dogisms

Trueue, dogs can't speak words. But some four-legged philosophers have wagged an enlightening thought or two.

If your bark is worse than your bite, then you're not biting hard enough.

— Moose (a.k.a. Eddie, the Jack Russell terrier on NBC's *Frasier*)

Did you hear the one about the dyslexic agnostic insomniac? He stays up all night wondering if there really is a doG.

— Anonymous

I don't know much about art, but I know what I lick.

— Moose

Some days you're the dog, some days you're the hydrant.

— Unknown

A dog is the only thing on earth that loves you more than he loves himself.

— Josh Billings

Heaven goes by favor. If it went by merit, you would stay out and your dog would go in.

— Mark Twain

Index